Love Endlessly
A Book of insight to inspire.

Book Cover Art by Luis Stefanell

In Native American Tradition, the Thunderbird
is the bearer of Happiness

Copyright by Luis Stefanell 2014©
All Rights Reserved
Decatur, Georgia

404-377-3112

Luis Stefanell
P.O. Box 692
Decatur, Georgia 30031

Dedicated to my parents

Mr. Renaldo Stefanell De la Rosa and

Mrs. Eufemia Isabell Vargas

In Loving Memory to both of my brothers:

Renaldo Stefanell, Jr.

And

Pepito Jose Stefanell

Thank you for your interest in this book. There are many ways to look at things, we have endless options. I'm sure there's something that will resonate for you within this book. The material here is to be inspiring as well as informative, but mostly to be shared.

When things are going good, great then everything is fine. I would say that would be a good day. But everyday is different and in the low energy days we all could use some words, thoughts of inspiration.

Staying centered or getting centered is important in being effective in our lives. A proper mind-set is important in staying in tune, in harmony with ourselves and everyone.

How we relate to ourselves and others is what this book is about. It's to inspire and motivate and help create a sense of peace.

Your life may be fine right at this moment and things could be going well for you but time and circumstances present challenges to us all and it's good to get other perspectives about things.

I hope you will keep this book handy and refer to it at times but mostly if you find yourself at a low point, a low energy day where it might offer you some good food for thought. When we're at a low point of the day we may find ourselves in need of encouraging words. Insightful - inspiring thoughts can get us back on track, refresh and inspire us.

As a student of life there is value in refreshing ourselves with uplifting words of encouragement at points throughout the day.

Along the way I read in a book that said 'nothing sounds sweeter than the sound of your name'. I'll take that a step forward and say your thoughts do the same. How we think! So how we think, what we place in our minds does make a difference to us, toward us. Its effect can be subtle in its way, yet also powerful, motivating us one way or another.

Goodness rises to the surface! Interpret this as 'you see it'. Goodness can't be denied.

So when someone says the new saying of the day "How's everything going in your world" you might say. Everything is fine, just fine!

And once again thank you for your interest in this book, may it serve you well and inspire you.

Peace and Blessings!

I would like to take this moment to thank those who have blessed and supported me with their kindness and loving support through the years.

Your interest and caring support has made the difference in my life.

Thank you!

The most important moment in our lives is this very moment. Reflections of the past may appear in our minds, which are fine, one of many gifts for us.

But this very moment to be fully in it 'fully', is to be centered with no concern of what hasn't manifested as a wish or desire as we may have from time to time.

It's what we intend to create to keep us moving forward, that's what this book is about, or should I say, one of the reasons I share this book. For me there are many reasons.

To be honest not every day is a day full of Sunshine. But the Light within ourselves radiates outward as well as inward to draw others to us, guiding one another forward. I use this word forward a lot because like in music there is a phrase commonly used as a 'progression' to move forward musically speaking, songs move in a forward direction which is what our lives are about if you think about it. And that is by divine design.

It's known that our body, you could say, has two minds. A conscious and a subconscious mind- the remembering mind. For a moment, think about this (your mind) as a computer, information in, and information now stored until retrieved. The thing about it when you're feeling good or well, it's easy naturally to think and speak positively and uplifting.

The same is said for the opposite. When down or at a low point it can be easy to draw upon the negative thoughts depending on the influences. And if not aware of the subtle negative energy one may be visiting, it can take us deep into further negative thinking, whatever might be on the surface of the subconscious mind stored. Until you may bring yourself right on down into the depths of depression, and as you may know there are different reasons for depression. A low grade of thinking and feeling isn't as affective for ourselves as when we are in a positive mind-set.

The understanding of this concept has been around for quite sometime. This book is my take on it as well as other thoughts, my views through my mind's eye, from my experiences.

There will always be someone who will step forward with the same message to share but only in a slightly different way. There will always be a need for this type of material. Man is either aware or not, fully conscious or not. And at times we make the wrong choice in communicating and aren't as effective as we could be.

We all have a desire to contribute to life as we know it. A desire to offer something of value that will serve others along their way, because Life supports Life.

It's not about the Quantity of Life, it's about the Quality of Life.

I live by word, Pure Spirit Yes, and that's a given. Anything of a positive nature written of value. For me the sayings I create hold some of the most truth as well, value, power. Why? Because they're mine, my thoughts and because this is my blessed Life that I have worked to understand and be as effective as I can while here moving forward contributing to all.

Good thoughts, good family and friends, good food, good air, are all good for a good Life!

By the way, the short one lines or short sentences that you have just read are known as affirmations. These thoughts, lines, sentences can be powerful to re-recite and over a period of time will stick to your subconscious-bio-computer mind. If the concept is new to you and you have an 'open mind' as they say, they will become part of your thinking naturally offering you energy and an uplifting of your spirit or your vibe, vibration.

In moments of frustration it can be easy to say things we don't really wish to say, if so, stop and take a breath and gather your thoughts, then speak. Just this sentence can offset and can eliminate any further damage in communication with another if and when the moment is heated.

In seeking a change of Life, of being, know it will have to start with a fresh mental outlook. Your view of yourself and others will come into play. Our thoughts and our words spoken can lead the way. Everything is enhanced by investing a little time and energy consistently. Nature knows the way we should go if we follow. Consistency is key to all new ventures.

Fear not that which you may not understand. Ask questions? Don't bother trying to read in between the lines, for you will surely miss the given message. The point of focus is the message. At times we humans try to make more of what is, than what 'really is' and throw ourselves off track and maybe assume things.

The idea here within this book is to have a plan, a way, a guide, call it what you will rather than to be clueless about the concept of the workings of the mind and the power of thoughts and words on us. Affirmations are powerful, so careful how you think and speak for you lay your own bricks to walk upon.

For me personally Spiritual work is important to keep my visions clearly in view; to offer me the Peace I seek and to be as effective as a person I can be. It offers me the connectedness to myself and others. It bears a sweet fruit.

Speak your mind as to whatever you desire but realize the difference towards the outcome will be determined by your input in the conversation, whether it be a self thought or a conversation with someone else. Your energy! Our effectiveness in communicating makes all the difference in all communication.

Bear in mind that no one is always perfect! Everyone is always on a path of some kind. We are all a work in progress-striving to get it right or better for ourselves and for others.

It's never too late to start something new you may be interested in. Consider the time factor. Something may have to be sacrificed in creating time needed to venture into a new area like the television or radio. Time allotted spent there is a good place to start to find and create extra time. Cutting out some of the shows or programming you may not really care about helps to create the time needed to be devoted to a creative endeavor- the arts, meditations, sports, music and so on. The things that can make a difference in our lives positively are the ones we should pursue. It's never too late to start something new!

Everything is of a choice nature

PONDER THE THOUGHT:
___
___
___

What may seem like inner or outer meaningless influences on you could be the greatest hold back in moving forward with the flow of your life. From the company we may keep, to the language we allow around us it all does make a difference.

Time seeking for better ways to be is time well spent!

A renewed outlook starts with keeping the house in order. Getting rid of old useless things no longer needed 'ways'- thoughts is the best place to start. New hopeful desired thoughts and wishes, positive thinking will bring results. Creating them is the power we all have using a focused mind. Accepting an open mind with new concepts makes the difference. With patience new things will appear in your life.

I give thanks in everything, for everything good!

Every little bit I do is that much more!

My beliefs are my sacred thoughts!

A BRIEF NOTE:

Some thoughts or sayings will reappear because of 'the word' the use, the power of them within this book.

Consider creating a Journal. A book to refer to and relate to with whatever is on your mind- whatever is in your heart. Express joy, thoughts, desires, loves, hurts, whatever is on your mind when you find yourself needing to be expressive- Express!

This is one of the most powerful ways to get out that which is on the surface of your mind- one of the most powerful ways to get in touch with yourself. Much can be worked out and solved using this simple concept. You will find in time that you will in fact offer a solution to a possible dilemma, or discover that it offers you an outlet to release thoughts and feelings.

The difference in succeeding is trying!

Learn to see the unseen Positively!

Every good thing in Life is earned!

There's an order to everything. Stick to first things first. However that is for you. Major concerns first, then address the other lesser things and details needing attention. Don't try tackling everything at once. You will find that when you move at a certain pace you don't forget anything. Also realize that when we rush we try to double step time and put a half hearted concentration into something important we need to do. Something may not be fully met.

Reawaken the passion within that may have fallen asleep!
Want it? . . . ask for it. . . receive it . . . and it's yours!

I enjoy the goodness I see in life, in others!

I am always learning and growing!

I believe of all that we possess nothing is more powerful than our Love! Once again I would add to that, our thinking. It really can't be mentioned enough, but I do within this book because of the subtleties of mindful, sometimes shifted thinking. What might be at times overlooked or not fully considered will make a big difference in our lives-awareness towards thinking.

Find your power, empower someone else out of Love!

Find your voice, speak it, enjoy it, and use it wisely!

Look at words simply, even deeply!

I am the Peace I seek. I create it!

I simplify Life in all areas!

People are happy!

Love is in the air!

Life's good!

Life is how we see things, the past, the now, the future. To create what we want for ourselves we must envision that which we aspire to manifest. See it in our mind's eye. Construct it as we wish for it to be. Define it with clarity. Consider before rest, or bedtime, think it through and simply express that which you desire. Allow your sub-conscious to gather this information and let it sink in deeply into your mind, your being.

My faith in myself is strong knowing all is and will be well no matter what life hands me!

My mind and heart are willing to consider other ways to serve me!

I now am open to new ideas!

Life is full of options!

We all have an inner conversation within ourselves whether we are aware or not. This is why it is always important to offer ourselves rest, vacation, hobbies, creative things of interest~ meditations, mental exercises to quiet the mind and offer a break from the constant inner conversation.

Discovering other ways of clearing my mind I know will make a difference!

I choose to think the best always!

I am aware of my thinking!

Life is a Blessing!

Being aware of the good around us has a very powerful place in our lives. Looking, and if one is to judge it should be reflective on the positive side of things. Reflect on the goodness you take in from your vantage point. Remember the inner conversation? The choosing the positive or negative thought, reflections? It is all a choice matter, always. No one places thoughts in our minds but ourselves, we are all responsible for our own thoughts.

My focus is on being Peaceful, Loving, kind even toward myself as I am Toward others.

Now I see the good results of being still and quiet.

Negative judgements have no real value to me.

What we send out we directly own for ourselves— be it whatever it will be. Taking the opportunity to change or incorporate new ideas will make a difference. We all self guide ourselves as we move along in life.

It feels good to make an effort to make my Life better.

I look forward to sharing this with others.

I say "Yes to Life"

_____

_____

_____

When someone cares and wants to give you a gift, something of a good nature, consider accepting it gladly out of kindness. Being open to accepting gifts is a gift to the giver. Giving is a big part of life in which we have all been given to. It makes the giver feel good and know something special has taken place.

Nothing could be more powerful than to move, touch the heart of another.

I gladly accept that which makes a difference to all.

Passion moves the Hearts

We are Blessed.

Understanding our own personal Nature is important. Being honest with how we see ourselves helps us understand the lives of others. If I find myself in harsh judgment of another, I place myself in their shoes and consider seeing things through their eyes.

Taking just a moment more to catch our thoughts can make a big difference for all.

We all deserve the highest regard of one another, toward one another.

I guide my thoughts well.

Life is a Blessing not a struggle. Moving along "freely" in positive thought and not feeling pulled down about unfortunate circumstances, challenges we all face is what we strive for.

Avoiding negative thoughts is a must. Due to exposure in this area, old ways, old self, this is important to consider. Thinking deeply about this life, not only ours but the lives of others and their challenges is what this life is about.

It is all in the giving, and hanging in there and realizing taking time to think things through patiently that there are ups and downs for everybody.

I am here to create, co-create a better life for myself and all.

Peace and patience are mine.

_____

_____

_____

You are what you think. We are as Powerful or as week as our thoughts. Considering the information within this book and incorporating these thoughts and ideas in our lives will make a difference.

Awareness is key for success; self-awareness connects us to co-awareness of others.

Life is managed best kept simple pure in spirit.

There is a solution for everything

I guide my thoughts.

Listen to your intuition, your inner voice of good reason. Not only that voice but all of all your being, it should resonate with "I am feeling, thinking like this", or however, whatever your message is in a moment.

I don't deny "how I feel, or think" within myself at this moment.

Find; create balance in all you do. Think-Work-Rest-Play.

Good results come from good actions.

Staying 'true to yourself' offers fulfillment- a fulfillment of knowing that you are on track with your life moving forward. Moving forward in life with the least amount of baggage is the most desired way to be.

I am empowered. . . I am self, Empowered.

We all are on our path.

My faith I draw upon.

I Live and let Live.

_____

_____

_____

The saying is "it takes a village to raise a child." I say keep your mind fresh and open to new and different concepts. It's easy and at times natural to just get used to the same old routine, the same way of doing things. Be daring to change things up and be free flowing as not to feel like you're automatic.

It takes a child's mind to wake up the village, the village within.

Things seem new in my life and exciting.

Life is good, my life is going well.

I am open to consider new ideas.

Leave your mark here and don't get hung up on any one part or aspect of your life by not attending to other areas needing attention. Managing ourselves requires a good game plan- a focus.

It feels good to know I am in command of my life. I guide it well.

I know all that I can do will make a difference.

Compare yourself to nobody in the negative sense of this thought. See your growth over a period of time and move more towards that. Trying to keep up with someone else really isn't the best choice, you are who you are with your own visions and timing and others are concerned with their visions as to 'how to do things' for themselves. You may be left behind following someone else neglecting your own intuition as your guide.

I now see the advantage of keeping my focus on my personal affairs.

I accept my life as is and handle myself to the best of my ability.

Understand that constant criticizing others may eventually lead to condemning others. We all deserve to receive the kindness and respect of others. Learning to let go and "let things roll off of our backs" and let things work themselves out is best.

I now choose to be more patient and develop more self respect.

We all are equal living out our lives differently.

I now choose to be more fair to others.

Prosperity for different people can mean different things. For some it may mean wealth, while for others it may mean fulfillment and peace of mind. Striving to do the best one can for me means first understanding one's personal nature well and starting from there to be and live with harmony contentedly.

I am not concerned with that which I don't have because I am focused on that which I do possess.

My life has been and is now prosperous in many ways.

I am thankful for my blessings.

When we look at ourselves as an instrument of love amazing things begin to happen. Realizing we have the power to evoke the most powerful positive emotion within others is more valuable than gold. Going through the motions of life can at times become seemingly automatic. Stepping out of that box and living closer to truths is actually more meaningful for us individually- requires a personal faithful spirit.

Touching and moving the hearts of others brings me joy.

My love and kindness will make the difference.

Nothing is more powerful than love.

Envision the outcome you desire to a situation time and time again. See it in your mind's eye coming into fruition, it manifesting itself to your desire. We create our world as we desire it to be. Your energy and power is valid just as you know you're reading this in this moment. Claim it, own it, and share it as your contribution to mankind.

I now see my desires manifesting "for" me.

My energies and power are to serve.

This is my life, my world to support.

Life is a gift!

Anger is one of the most important negative emotions to conquer, to control. It can take away from our good energy. It's all a moment-to-moment thing, how am I feeling, thinking . . . how am I reacting?

It can rob the Spirit of precious energy and Love that can be directed toward others or one self to get things done. Frustration is understandable to deal with. Venting in positive ways has its benefits. The Spirit will generate even more of what exist. So anger and frustration should be managed.

I know I don't have to respond or react to everything I hear or see!

I can save my Peace for as long as I have to.

I realize that what is important, I should save my attention and not waste my Good energy being a constant Reactive person!

Toxic energy comes in many forms. Learn to see it. If it's outside of yourself you may not have complete control over it. If it's within you, 'your thoughts', you have complete control over it if you choose to do so. Examine your thinking, consider all thoughts. If it is coming at you, you don't have to respond to it. Step aside and let it pass you by. You don't have to react to everything, save your power!

One must understand disorder to understand order. Everything follows a path.

I don't worry or concern myself with things I can't control outside of me!

I peacefully go within to find Truth, Spirit, guidance for this moment!

No one has the power to control me, only I do with Love!

I won't get caught up in the Negative Web of Life!

I strive for the inner understanding of things!

My serenity is with me all day long!

I don't dwell on things negatively!

Hate is a powerful negative word in my mind. Just as all words are powerful depicting one thing or another. This is not an everyday word I use, the fact is I seldom use it if at all, but only at a time like this I will describe the following.

Hating can lead to more hating. My belief is in conversation, its subtle use, over a period of time one can work themselves in a corner of hating this and that and on and on. I have substitute words to describe what I am saying, and that's for my benefit, for the reasons I just mentioned.

Who I used to be is who I used to be. Who I am now is the most important thing to me now . . . in this moment!

I forget and release the negative events of yesterday!

My actions tell who I am. My words reveal my heart!

I draw from my positive thoughts, my thinking!

I am in control of my Blessed Life always!

It is my intention to stay positive!

I give others the benefit of doubt!

Life is Good!

During challenging times we must learn new ways to adapt. Which means adopting a new approach toward things. Which means to change in some way to some degree. Be daring in your Life. Nothing comes to us by just wishing for it (or wishing for something to change). Reach for it . . . create it!

It's not what we don't have in life, it's what we have and how we use it that matters!

Faith is knowing a positive action will take place soon even at this very moment!

If anything is to get done it will be by our intention for it to be so. Our minds lead the way!

Being persistent is never allowing outside or inner forces to influence you to give up on what you want or need, or desire in Life!

*Insecurities can be turned around
with insight and guidance!*

*Self improvement is a
moment-to-moment thing!*

Never let what 'you think' others are negatively feeling or thinking about you, affect you. After all, your thinking may only be your thinking. Why choose to get caught up in a hopeless scenario- or an assumption, if you will? Move forward with your positive thoughts of yourself and circumstances which need your attention. If we constantly keep a positive thought in our mind and negative influences out, we function much more effective.

Positive energy moves things forward. Negative energy holds things back. Both can filter into other areas of our lives making a difference one way or another. This is why it's important to be aware of all energies and thoughts, as well.

Learn to read the body language of others as well as your own. Keep your head to the sky or keep your head up is a very good saying. It has its place in helping the confidence within! We guide ourselves along in life, we're independent thinkers and doers.

Negative assumption thinking kills a positive Spirit. It sabotages a good Spirit!

It takes a good energy to Live a good life!

I am focused!

Spirit is Life Force Energy moving through every living thing. It doesn't rest that's one reason it has to be guided in some way to be effective. Creative Spirit doesn't rest. We are just that- Creative Spirits! There's a time to think, to guide, and to just be.

Just as we have been taught and guided, we guide ourselves along in Life setting the path for ourselves. Much of the information within this book focuses on just that . . . shining a light on the working affects of our minds-our thinking process.

The saying is time heals everything! The process is sped up, accelerated, when a concentrated intentional Loving, Peaceful, thoughtful energy exist!

How we relate to ourselves and others is important in our lives!

We are all different . . . but we are all alike also.

Lead with your heart, guide your mind!

Life is good!

Harsh judgment of others only robs the good spirit. It takes much of our own good energy and could possibly cast someone in an unfair light. Having opinions about things, circumstances, encounters, is natural, but getting caught up in harsh-negative judgments is something to keep an eye on and consider– to what degree and how critical for how long? It is something to be aware of.

A choice of higher thought will bring about higher results!

Letting your Love Light shine, is giving of your heart!

We are one another's keeper!

Complain less and do more!

Care what you think!

I believe the inability to communicate effectively can be the beginning to the end. We are either drawn to one another or not, whether it is a personal friendship or a business relationship. I know 'this may sound' a bit drastic but it is the truth. Our ability to communicate clearly and effectively makes the difference.

I am becoming more aware of the importance of my energies!

Life doesn't have to seem like a struggle; it flows effectively!

The best choices are made when I am calm!

I don't have to force anything in Life!

I know it is all give and take.

_____

_____

_____

Personally, I understand the concept of speaking about religion or spirituality is not always necessary and at times should be avoided. Many can get caught up in another's belief system and allow their beliefs to get in the way of something that could be special. Whether it be a personal or business relationship, I know that this is a sacred space for all. It is never for me to harshly consider, criticize another's sacred space- whatever that may be. I understand that we are much more liberal and outspoken now in this time. But for a more higher reason and values we should consider this area of our beings and be selective as to when, with whom or even to what degree to allow ourselves to engage in this area of conversation. Unnecessary walls can be built when too much is revealed freely.

I respect the sacred space of others and don't allow myself to be intrusive!

I don't have to engage in anything or everything about my personal life with everyone!

Life flows just fine taking care of my affairs, looking after my interest!

Everyone deserves the space and time to be as they are!

My needs are met when I guide myself effectively!

I can be an inspiration to others by my actions!

Nature knows the way it should go if we follow!

Spirit, Dios, God, Creator has created a life of endless options for me to draw from. I co-create this wonderful Life I lead myself through. My Life has meaning. As some may at times question my Life-direction, my path, I know who I am and move at my pace not competing with anyone for any reason in the area of my spirituality. I keep my focus on my affairs knowing this is my sacred space.

Positive thoughts and words guide my path!

I am taking charge of my Life!

I force nothing in Life!

I guide my thoughts!

Consider the concept of being or living in a 'Fearless or Fear-based' way. Think about this for a moment. Think about how this may be one way or the other- two distinctly different concepts with their own power. One is purely positive with it's own Life Force Energy moving forward knowing it will succeed and the other just not sure of itself. Confidence isn't arrogance, it is a self assured energy of knowing even if going into the unknown; it's all going to be fine.

If what I have planned doesn't manifest for me, I know things will work out fine!

My concern is laying solid bricks to walk upon in Life!

The less I use the word 'Fear' the better off I am!

My Life Force Energy starts with my thinking!

Things are starting to shift well for me!

Fearless is a concept I understand!

I live and let live!

Just as with any plant, it begins with a seed. Seeds slowly start to grow. Our thoughts do the same. The positive ones also depending where your spirit is (how you feel, think) the negative ones do the same. This is important to consider always.

I see the positive results of my good intentions now!

I Bless this day! I Bless this day in every way!

I am open to realizing many of these truths!

I am positive and kind to all.

I say 'All the best'! a lot because that is how I care to speak. My mind wants to reflect on the Goodness Naturally, and I realize the importance of it. As co-creator of my life, I am thankful for this season of my Life. So I say . . . 'All the best'!

I act on that which feeds my positive spirit, I know there's a reason it is within.

I guide my mind and give of my heart!

My thoughts are powerful!

Life is a blessing!

Understanding that depression is a treatable disease is very important. It starts in the mind. How we think, and feel emotionally about ourselves and things in general is extremely important to keep up with because it's a known fact things are moving a bit faster in time. Have you noticed how much faster people are speaking these days?

This is a good place to see how easy it is to misunderstand someone, or be misunderstood in conversation. With important matters make it a point to hone in on your timing to get your views across clearly.

The positive changes I see within myself are welcomed!

I enjoy the goodness I see in others!

I am the Peace I seek!

All is well!

Never underestimate how quickly you can turn something around for the better. It is a concept of time, are we patient enough? Are we realistic giving it 'its proper time' to change. Being patient has its value.

Spirit goes into the unknown faithfully!

Peacefully I can handle any situation!

I am fully in this moment, aware!

What comes in or what we bring into our minds affects us, it affects us all one way or another. Subtle thoughts should be considered just as any strong passionate thought. Reflect on this for a moment. Taking time is always best when working out our dilemmas that arise. Sit on it if you have to. Sleep on it when important decisions have to be made and require more time.

Cultivate your Highest Thoughts and share them. See the effect they have on others. Song writers do this all the time. They express their 'Truths', stories within a song. The positive thoughts one expresses in a diary or journal are the most powerful, one way or another.

Everyone wants to hear something beautiful, hopeful and uplifting!

At times think with your heart and feel with your mind!

I trust in life, I trust in my Life, all is well!

Live well! Well enough to accept your life as it is and being grateful for it! Like your life as it is! Work well! Well enough to know what you have done will make the difference as to your contribution towards life-to fellow man. Live in a way to know that you're doing the best you can for yourself and others. Know that you are on your path just as others are, moving forward progressively, peacefully forward.

Help someone to achieve the same of what they need for themselves. One of the greatest parts of Living is Giving!

I enjoy sharing because I know it makes a difference!

I celebrate all that's meaningful to me!

Confidence and courage leads me well!

Life is good. God is Good!

The nature of man's spirit is to endure. It is to stay engaged hanging on faithfully knowing that it is by its nature to do so. I believe there are things for us to know and things for us to discover. In my mind, some things should be and are a mystery. And I'm perfectly fine with that. I don't need to know everything but I do need to flow with all that is good. If you think about this we all do individually, we have, and we will forever more.

The curiosity of man naturally guides him to the mysteries of life to discover all.

Things don't happen to me. They happen for me!

To understand and grow is my Life!

There is no limit to my life's experiences!

In my heart is the Love for all beings!

The Universe operates in fine perfect order. If things don't work out for me as planned, to my desire, I'll wait for the next best thing, the surprise that will take its place. My Peace allows for everything to fall into place Naturally! I don't force things.

Our intuition guides us all day long. Our good, cultivated inner voice is always guiding us along!

I am free to accept all the goodness Life has to offer me right now!

I visualize what I want to manifest in my Life now!

Life has endless options!

Place yourself on the line- whatever that means for you. Whether it's your Love, your work, your friendships. Give yourself the chance to express yourself and not feel paralyzed by not allowing your voice to be heard. It's all in how we communicate with ourselves. It makes a big difference!

A friend will always take the time to listen to another friend. Kind support is enough and can make the difference to anyone. Letting some vent for themselves is very useful and a gift you give them. It only cost a little time and attention.

Be open to other people's opinions and thoughts. Look for the positive in them.

When listening to someone, listen with all your body, all your being!

I am considerate towards others!

Trust is earned!

Daring to be different will require you to simply be yourself. It will require detaching, in some ways, what 'you think' others may think of you. Move along peacefully being effective lovingly.

Any good idea I consider to follow up on I realize is of a High order, a godly nature.

Success for me isn't what I achieve it's who I strive to be!

Confidence is very different from arrogance!

This is a new day to receive all that is good!

Eventually things always work out. What may have been difficult today will be different tomorrow. Slowly in time the difficult days seem to get behind us as we see things in a different light. We humans tend to get very impatient and want instant change. But all of nature changes at its own pace– some things faster than others.

Eventually answers to questions and dilemmas will appear when you have patience. It's gratifying as our minds bond with our hearts with positive thoughts!

Focus on the positive. Disregard the negative!

My faith is constantly growing!

Things always work out!

Work toward that which you want to be your life's work. Find a way to make it happen! It will make a big difference as to how you feel about your life, about things in general. Realize that some things have a certain time span and as we change our work interest, change will come about as well. Making shifts into other areas is natural and at times necessary. Different interests serve us in our personal lives.

Our well being isn't just a matter of good health--work plays a big part of the picture.

The most important person holding you back in life could be yourself.

The future will bring me what I desire because I plan for it!

My inner self speaks to me all the time. I listen!

Free yourself from yourself!

Consider what constant second guessing yourself may offer you. The back and forth of not being sure of yourself could stir up confusion in your mind. Getting calm and centered is the answer- then go from there.

I understand that constant training is the only way to attain strategy. Consistency is key!

I consider all facts and always choose the best decision concerning important matters!

I am responsible for my circumstances. I don't blame anyone or myself!

With Peace I give thanks for all good.

I take full responsibility for myself!

Trust in the good spirit we are given. Trust in the faith you have. Trust in the goodness you place in your heart and mind! As for me, what we do here as our work, our livelihood, is important in the way of our work, but who we are and what we're here for has a deeper meaning.

Peace and joy are found in an effective mind!

A disciplined mind creates balance!

My life has profound meaning!

Trust in your intuition!

Uncertainty is also a path to freedom. Freedom comes with a small price of knowing that going into something that may seem uncertain will work out well in its own way because of the faith we place in it.

Stepping into the unknown can also be viewed as 'this will also be fine' because I will make it so!

Our brains, minds, our thinking are primary to our beings. My work doesn't lead me to my mind. My mind leads me to my work, my livelihood!

I have accomplished much in my life and more is yet to come!

With gratitude I give thanks for my blessings!

I am in charge of my thinking!

Life is good.

Follow your Bliss! Whatever that means for you! Cultivate your highest thoughts! Give thanks for every good thing that moves you deeply. Find peace and see the beauty in everything and everyone. Keep it pure and simple . . . Just Love!

I see the good results of the spiritual work I am doing!

I am here to Love no matter who, what or where I am!

My offerings bless all that welcome me in!

Peace and Love guide me!

All is well!

Learn to let go of concerns at the end of the day's work. Your higher self works even at the time of your rest, working out and offering ideas and solutions to possible dilemmas needing attention. As we age, this becomes more important, letting things go and shifting into a relaxed mode naturally, releasing tension and stress is important.

You will find that you are not missing out on anything, quite the contrary, it is more the truth. You will realize that you will have more energy to meet the demands you take on. Energy has to come from somewhere. It's found in different types of rest. For me personally I run on energy reserve which serves me well.

We are our best healers. Read, think, pray, rest! Anything that gives you energy and re-energizes you, do it often. Consistency is key!

The inner mind tells itself what it really wants to hear- what it knows to be true, something kind, loving and giving in Nature.

'Blind faith' is moving forward peacefully knowing your desires, your needs will be met!

Being at Peace is knowing that all is being taken care of, even in this moment!

I take care of myself, I guide myself well!

I am responsible for my well being!

Some would say money is power. I say peace is power! Information and knowledge is the power which creates peace. Money doesn't buy everything you need or may want but Peace can bring you understanding to everything!

I know who I am. I know where I am and where I am going. From goodness I came, the goodness I give, my life is focused!

I accept all the goodness life offers me now and always!

Be open and receptive to new ideas!

I am blessed!

Go out of your way to be helpful when you can. Never under estimate any good action or intention you may share with another. Its reach could go further than you'll ever know!

I understand that life isn't just about all the wonderful things I experience myself. But I also recognize that others are on their path moving forward in Life. Any good thought I can share I know will make a difference in someone's Life.

Compassion is the fashion!

I send others light and Love!

I am here to serve!

Today will be a good day! A productive day! Only I determine what that means to me. I will accomplish much this day and that which doesn't get taken care of will be taken care of tomorrow.

Self regulation is within everything, all of Life. It regulates itself as time moves along. We all do the same. Every living thing does!

My Life is timeless! My focus is here and now, this moment!

I take it one day at a time!

Imagine circumstances from the other person's view point. Consider that before making any drastic decisions about a situation. Understanding why someone is or why they may be a certain way is important and useful in relationships. Putting yourself in someone else's shoes and taking the time to understand others is very important.

Depending on the circumstances some people deserve one, two, three, maybe even four or more chances to be treated fair toward them and to ourselves!

I overlook nothing regardless of its seemingly insignificance!

Care for things, Love people!

All hearts are connected!

Tolerance is cultivated!

Go out of your way to say hello to someone first! People at times tend to be reserved. Don't anticipate rejection. Instead see that it may be your shyness that could make a difference in meeting someone new. Put yourself out there!

Blessings are to be shared– anything of a good nature should be shared in some way . . . And that would be you!

Let those who you care for feel important. Let them know you are interested in their lives!

Life is a Dance . . . learn to move in all directions with ease!

Live fearlessly . . . Love endlessly!

A kind word goes a long way!

Give out of the Spirit of Love!

Just like some of the world's beautiful diamonds, we are created under great pressure. At times we are to endure and can, providing we take good care of ourselves. We owe ourselves and others the benefit of doubt.

It's easy to wonder, then to question, then, maybe, to arrive at a conclusion, then perhaps judge others, maybe harshly judge others. Like the saying goes, 'don't judge a book by its cover'. We can at times be a bit too quick to do this.

Complaining, criticizing, condemning serves no one. It is a wasted energy. Time is better spent towards any positive creative endeavor!

Look for the goodness in others, see it, give thanks you found it!

Happiness is found in a heart less burdened!

Keep a light heart!

Never underestimate the smallest thing, thought, you could share with another. The impact it can have on them could make all the difference to them.

A renewed outlook is the start to a new lease on Life! Everyone deserves the change they may be seeking!

Everything is in an exchange of some sort. All life is in motion, alive and thriving on its own.

Some things don't have to be said, just shown with a pure heart!

My focus is on being Loving and Kind to all!

I claim my good!

Be aware of the mood you may be in. At times when our energies are low, our moods, our emotions change. If not pleased with what's in the moment mood wise, get centered and shift into a mood that is pleasing- where you feel balanced, positive, focused, and effective!

We are our best healers when we act on our higher thoughts!

Isolation isn't anybody's friend. In some way we must circulate. Everything is always in movement.

When centered and balanced we are in a better place to be inspired. Everything comes naturally to us when we are relaxed and upbeat.

All good thought's lead to good places!

Much is learned by observing!

I am centered!

We all have the same joys and sorrows— losses in life. It's all in how we deal with the sorrows and possible setbacks that makes the difference. Moving through this type of period only allows us to get back on track and enjoy the joys of life that much more.

Being optimistic requires faith knowing this energy gets things done! It's a matter of choice, a positive mind set.

My moments have been interesting. I am so blessed to be right where I am in my life now!

All past events, affairs, are behind me now. My focus is on being here, now, with gratitude!

I focus on the quiet and Peace that surrounds me in this moment!

There are no problems, only solutions!

Being understanding and tolerant of other's beliefs is what anyone would like. You don't have to engage or encounter an exchange and at times it's a better call not to. Just being a good listener is operating from a respectful place.

There is a time to think, a time to listen, a time to look and a time to just be– also, a time to smile!

Children need guidance, adults need patience, elders need compassion– all need love!

Out of respect, be open to another person's ideas and thoughts!

We all are equally Divine!

Be aware of possibly falling into the judgmental trap. The useless act of judging others harshly and maybe on every least little thing, is not being aware of your own energies, which could be put to good use. Judging others builds walls and can interfere with relationships.

Everyone has their own truths, beliefs. We should respect everyone for their beliefs.

Their beliefs are theirs and your beliefs are just that, yours! We don't have to agree with someone to be at peace with others or ourselves.

Time is valuable and my affairs must be taken care of before getting caught up negatively in the lives of others!

I am and always will be a student of Life! There is always something new for me to learn in Life!

The only one we are fully in control of is ourselves, our thinking, our actions!

We don't have to be reactive to everything we see or hear!

Tolerance is cultivated!

There is a lot of truth in cliché sayings. As a mental exercise, write out a few and offer your interpretation as to what they mean to you, your definition. Adopt positive sayings from wherever you may see them- the shorter the better.

You could go to songs and pick up so may positive phrases like "I can see clearly now"... that I'm looking at things differently... or ... "What a difference a day makes" ... after resting and letting things just go. Remember the idea of this book is about our thinking!

There are different ways we convey a story situation to ourselves and to others. Thinking and acting out our lives is something once again what this material book is about. For me this is my offering for all.

I value what I strongly believe in, therefore if I deem it good and in this season of my life, I simply want to share my thoughts.

My life is so much more than I may realize, a big part of it is to explore and discover!

Change, if need be in some way, may be the call. By the way, we all have since birth answered the calls it's just that staying connected to all of our being can have its challenges at times and life marches on, all the more to 'stay connected'.

Everything is taking on a newness now that I am taking good care, things feel new!

I am getting better in touch with all of myself starting with my thinking!

Life is full of endless options!

Another idea to consider is to start journal writing. It's a powerful way to get in touch with your thoughts. The act of reading and writing effects many areas of your life and throughout all your life.

All words carry their own weight. Take time in conveying your thoughts!

Profess your beliefs, your truths, as to what you know what to be true. Write them out and re-read them from time to time— even daily!

Consider writing poetry— it's something I call 'pretzel logic'. It can make you dig deep in thought working your mind, expanding your thinking.

There's no such thing as a wasted effort for any thing . . . maybe it's just a lost opportunity not taken.

Peace is found in a calm heart, a spirit centered in Love!

I imagine it to be fun just to write something!

I'm not in a hurry to convey my thoughts!

It's never late to start something new!

Being creative is a natural thing!

Offer yourself another chance. Another try at something you desire is something you deserve to do! When your energy and attitude is at a low point it's easy, perhaps, not to care as much, but we all deserve to offer ourselves another chance!

Giving up is easy while staying in the mix does offer gifts! It's all up to ourselves to decide as to what we choose to hear or what written material we choose to read, even that of my works here within this book. We don't have to agree with everything. But to be open and consider it, if it resonates, it should confirm itself within you.

Knowing and caring for myself and others is knowing the heaven within!

Keep the conquering spirit alive within!

Effort eventually brings results!

I say yes to Life!

We are all a work in progress! There's always a value for self improvement— that moment will make itself known. 'Life is good in many stages, in many phases' ! Life flourishes to the fullest, naturally.

If you keep doing what you're doing you are only going to have just that! We are creatures of habit, but we are meant to change. We are meant to incorporate interest that keep us feeling new and refreshed— to keep a clear outlook on life of things in general.

Change could require just doing one new thing you always wanted to do. Or, for that matter, stop doing one thing your inner good voice, spirit, is telling you to stop doing.

Envision how you want your life to be. Do this often knowing and faithfully that your vision will manifest for you that it's happening right now, in this moment. Be patient and practice waiting for the results.

What we have when we strip everything away we begin to see the true beauty of 'Life is' what creation is and that we're a big part of it. We realize that we have a part in guiding Life's course, yes, even in seemingly small ways.

Thrive on! Let no one or any thing get in the way or hold you back in life, including yourself!

All of life flourishes to the fullest Naturally. It's a law of nature!

I flow with the course of my life Naturally!

Give away what you most value and watch what happens within you! As for me this would be my good thoughts, also my music. I enjoy touching a heart- moving someone deeply. I am grateful for the chance to help someone through a difficult time. Also I enjoy sharing the gift of music given to me. Think about the power you have to give— help heal!

Blessings are to be shared. Anything of a good nature should be shared freely in some way!

In some way we are one another's spirit guide!

Giving is getting, getting is giving!

Give out of the spirit of Love!

I am generous and giving!

Study your personal Nature and provide for it what it calls for. If you notice it will call for that which can't be bought with money. The saying is 'the best things in life are free'!

Don't let the negative events of the day get in your way. Better to be strong in mind, and sound in positive thoughts to help you create the kind of life you desire!

Make time to go out into Nature— a park, lake or just take a walk. The beach will provide the space we long to feel that we are a part of all the good that surrounds us.

When things seem to get a little crazy, slow down to understand and also to gain control of the situation!

My yesterdays are gone— this moment is here and now waiting for me to create my next moments!

The days may seem short, the years may seem shorter, but my Love last forever!

City life moves much faster than country life. Learn to balance both!

I see the beauty all around me— within me!

I take time to just be!

As an inner-outer relaxing exercise movement, stand with your arms next to your body, by your sides. Take one intentional breath in through your nose and at the same time slowly lift your arms only to shoulder height with palms (open hands) facing upward. Then slowly release your breath ex-hailing, lowering your arms back to sides of your body.

This should all flow naturally. Do this as many times as you like to relax. It is simple, yet very effective.

There will never be another moment like this one. I give thanks!

Honing in on your energy only expands your energy!

I release all tension and thoughts from my mind!

My body is always regenerating itself!

Spirit is the Life force energy moving through every living thing. It doesn't rest. That's one reason it has to be guided in some way to be effective. Creative spirit doesn't rest, we are just that 'Creative Spirits'.

Peace and love is found in the Hearts of those that seek it, also in the ones that may have forgotten it existed!

There's a time to be, also a time to just smile!

It's easier to maintain, than to get in shape!

Everything in Life has a balance– create it!

Romance life itself! Do this by taking even the simplest moments in your life that moves you deeply where you may find yourself even fixated on the sweet moments that once were.

Just as the saying goes "when one door closes, another door opens." One could say when one heart closes another one opens. Keep your heart and mind open!

Give something to someone at least once a day if it be only your good thoughts. If no one is around, give it to yourself and enjoy it for what it is!

My life is about being kind, loving, and giving to all!

Romance is key to Love!

Joy generates more joy!

If you look at a child's eyes you will see a sparkle within. It's the Love and wonderment of Life that has their attention. Everything is of that nature. Within that nature there is a faithful knowingness that more is yet to come. It's important to create that excitement! Hang on to it! The key word is create it!

I am not defined by what people may at times think or feel about me negatively. I am defined by what I place in my heart and mind and who I create myself to be!

Forgiveness towards others is of a high order. Every good thing is cultivated in Love!

The same goodness we see in others is found in ourselves!

To simply Love others brings gifts to your door!

Live fearlessly, Love endlessly!

Never lose the playful spirit towards Life. Study the joy and playfulness of children and place yourself in their minds, imagine how they must see things and how they're thinking.

Look, search for the magic, the mystery of Life. Children do this all the time. Adults seem to lose this quality, 'the creative spirit', as we get older.

Don't stop looking until you find that which moves you so much you have to go back again and again because it gives you so much energy and lifts your spirit!

Acting on your highest thoughts will offer fulfillment to others as well as to yourself!

Do the things you like, Love the things you do!

Be active in some way into your years!

Joy generates even more joy.

In the healing world there's a saying 'Stagnation is death, circulation is life'! To me, this applies to everything! When our energy's high or we're feeling positive and good about ourselves, everything is fine. We can't get enough wonderful Life!

We're not thinking of being low energized or negative or without or, for that matter, any number of the other ways we may feel. Things are magnified when we are ill, sick or when we're at a low point or when some dilemma presents itself.

Find ways to increase your energy. Energetic people attract people. Also, learn ways to conserve energy. Knowing how to pace yourself is valuable for all your life.

Read, Think, Pray, Rest!

_____

_____

_____

Do anything that gives you energy— that which re-energizes you!

You are unique! Nobody can Sing or Dance like you! No one can give or Love like you do! Celebrate your Life in all ways!

My life is constantly in movement— exciting things await me!

Praise, towards the slightest improvement goes a long way!

In time things always get better again!

Life is a gift!

The only obstacle I understand in moving me forward could be myself. So I just move forward Peacefully into the future, faithfully into the unknown knowing all will be fine and well for me.

I am a positive thinker! I am a positive energy- a Life-force energy doing what I'm here to do. Peacefully knowing that in the unknown answers, solutions to dilemmas are found there.

The main idea here is to know that not allowing any negativity into my being places me already ahead for any good thing ready to connect with me.

Good opportunities don't always come around. When a good one presents itself I consider taking it!

I am intellectual, light-hearted, humorous, faithful, sensual, kind, Loving, and giving. A spiritual being created out of Love!

I entrust my intuition to lead me well in Life!

I savor the simplest meals!

Emotions stir Passion!

Love is fearless!

Don't be paralyzed mentally when in a difficult situation or circumstance which at times present themselves. Clear your mind and act on your highest thought!

To some, unfortunate circumstances could be viewed as opportunities to learn from, as well as in all encounters. Take no harsh action in a moment of frustration, a moment of high emotion. Think totally through the consequences before taking action.

I don't impose or force myself on things I must have my way!

I always think things through carefully before deciding!

Be kind and courteous to all!

Tolerance is cultivated!

I accept the Godly good as is and work at changing anything that doesn't appear the same!

Write out your highest thoughts and expand on them, then act on them!

Desire, wish for what you want– work for what you need!

Cultivate reading and writing skills often!

If someone tells you that you can't do that great thing, thank them just the same and go and do that great thing anyway! Their power and outlook is theirs and yours is yours. Only you know what your good spirit calls you to do. Follow your intuition!

Persistence is a wonderful trait to have, it will make the difference in getting what someone wants or needs. Eventually getting what you need and desire will manifest!

With every 'no' there are two 'yeses' just around the corner!

I share all goodness with others!

I take responsibility for myself!

All change is inevitable. Naturally we aspire to grow and live out our lives peacefully loving harmoniously happy.

Playing it safe isn't always the answer, not answering the call for change. One might be uncomfortable with being willing to change. We're creatures of habit, wanting things to be constantly the same. 'The table goes here and the light goes here' and so on. We help ourselves move forward or we keep ourselves in the same place, is my message.

Our body, our mind, our total being, spirit, longs for change naturally. If you think about it we have in the past changed to a degree but it's my thought that one can easily get settled and lose the quality of flowing freely as we age. This could be because 'playing it safe' is the easiest thing to do.

The past is gone- it's history now! The most important time for me is this moment! The past is now behind me, I move forward with life!

Everything changes in time, difficult moments do come to pass. Being peaceful and centered helps guide me effectively!

Peace is the first and last answer to all things!

Life is full of many options!

If you want to change your personal world you should consider how you speak. The words we use keep us moving one way or another. Forward, backward or even standing still, giving ourselves hope, being forth coming in positive spirit is valuable as we move along.

Keep your home, living space, in order. When your space is cluttered your mind can take on the same vibration. Our surroundings do play a part on us, as well as how it impacts our minds. Organization— internally we want order and that would also apply to our living space.

A wise person knows that even one candle can light up a room. A candle light of love can light up a whole room full of Love!

To be human is to be spiritual, spirit is in every living thing!

Kindness is not weakness. The opposite is more the truth!

Staying centered or getting harmony with ourselves and with others.

Consider meditation classes. If you don't know or don't have a book to learn from to bring the mind and body together, schools and teachers are everywhere now. Meditation revitalizes and helps regenerate— it centers the body. It provides so much more for mind, body and spirit.

Being focused along with my self discipline and consistency will make the biggest difference for me!

I have the power to help me heal myself quickly, naturally!

I care for myself and other's well being— I give thanks!

Different day, same ole bliss!

How we think and speak leads our way, our path in life. All thoughts and words carry their own weight.

I have found many wonderful things in life. I am grateful and I look forward to more surprises to discover!

I am what I claim myself to be. I am defined by my mind's thoughts of who I am. I take ownership of myself as I guide myself through life by my thoughts.

I realize that everyone does the same— we are all connected!

Every little bit I do is that much more!

Peace, pace, and patience are mine!

I hope that you will keep this book handy and refer to it at times, mostly if you find yourself at a low point- that it may help inspire you in some ways. When we find ourselves at a low point we benefit from encouraging words. Insightful, inspiring thoughts can get us back on track.

Your life may be fine right where it is at this moment and things could be going well for you but time and circumstances present challenges to us all and it's good to have different perspectives about things in general.

Place a plant in the center of any room and it will grow toward the light source, towards the window, the light.

All life is as it should be– lessons are to be learned and at times relearned!

There are no problems, only solutions!

I can adapt myself to anything!

Every day is an opportunity for me to give thanks for my yesterdays! My attention is on being here now. My tomorrows haven't yet arrived but I patiently wait, this moment's just fine. So blessed am I to cross paths with the ones that have touched my life with their love and kindness. I call this my awakening dream. As fast as things may seem to go in my life I never want to stray from this wonderful place I am within.

I look for the good in people. I look for the loving kindness toward others and toward themselves. I look for the peace they possess and I smile within!

How we relate toward ourselves and others is what this book is also about.

There are no illusions here in life. Everything natural is real– alive!

Love is the only answer!

Love is fearless!

Trying to change someone is like trying to rearrange the clouds. Offering positive suggestions and insight with no pressure is more effective.

Giving someone a sense of hope can make the biggest difference in their life. Helping them create a new outlook will create a turnaround for them.

Take time to guide others seeking answers to life's questions, ways to arrive to peace and understanding. Speak in a calm voice even when frustrated. Never make a situation worse by over reacting!

Send light and love to those that seem unkind, unloving!

All life supports life!

Learning not to take things personal has it's advantages. Jumping to conclusions with possible negative assumption, serves no one. Think the best, be at peace!

It's important to recognize how we react to a situation. In control, out of control?

Don't make important decisions when frustrated or angry. Let time pass and choose the right moment to think things through clearly.

Eventually all gardens need weeding!

Discourage discouragement!

Time is what we have!

Take time to just be!

Compassion is of a high order- compassion for others as well as for ourselves. It's found in being loving. To be kind and loving to others is to know the same directly.

I say 'Truth is Golden'! We should hold out for all facts before even passing judgments, if at all, upon another. It takes a good energy to live a good life. A good energy to withhold because man at times is quick to rush to judgment and it serves no one.

I understand the act, the power of forgiveness. My being forgiving is a gift not only toward others but a gift to me that I create!

Listen intently to others with an open mind- it is all anyone would desire.

Avoid arguing- suggest discussing matters instead.

Peace is found created within!

Truth is Golden!

Handling ourselves in a peaceful manner helps make our journey here easier to navigate through this blessed life. But if ever needed, place yourself on the line and always speak your mind and express what you must. Remember, it's all in the way and the words you choose to speak that will make the difference in being effective.

Don't sit on your hands and give up your right to express yourself, ever!

Prayer and meditation at any point of the day, including daily reflections, makes a big difference in cultivating the peace we seek.

I am all the wonderful things and ways I wish to be!

Romance your desires, your dreams!

Freedom is for all to enjoy and not just for some. Find and fight for your freedom. I mean this in the sense that it's all in how you go about claiming what's yours to begin with; not hurting anyone in the process. How one goes about obtaining what they need is fight the good fight well!

Allow and empower others to find their own!

To me life is moving at a more upbeat pace in time. A major contributor is the internet brought to our door. Practice leaving it out for part of a day or all of a day if possible.

It's easy to fall into the creature of habit way of being. Thinking is good, fine, but just being and taking in all that's around us is a very profound experience. There is much to sense and feel as well.

Take a walk or go to a park. The color green is the meditative color. It's all around us. Instantly tranquilizing and relaxing. Stay centered, in touch with your inner self which is the in-ter-net!

When needed, breath slowly inward through your nose and exhale out of your mouth when frustrated or angered. It's naturally relaxing. The effect is immediately calming.

Yoga is one of the best forms of exercise which requires little effort. It re-centers the body bringing mind and body as one. The word Yoga means 'union'. Taking pressure off of joints, nerves, and muscles provides so much more.

One of the best ways to learn something is to teach it, pass it along!

I am in control of myself, my well being and I wish the same for all!

Being at peace is creating it!

Pursuing creative interest, adventures, requires a daring heart. One that is focused on the journey knowing the joy of the adventure awaits you. It's never too late to start something new!

Creative people soon learn that everything ever created is recreated in other unique, new exiting ways!

Developing creative interest gives you something to look forward to tomorrow. The things we make and do offer us a natural diversion from the normal day-to-day things we do. The stimulation does serve mind and body well.

Creative people live with the excitement of forming things that move them as well as others. Creative endeavors provide a positive interests, an outlet to see things through. Having something to look forward to tomorrow is important. It offers a certain power which carries over into other areas of our lives.

Positive interests, ideas are all around us. Always carry a pen to capture good ideas!

Everything is coming to me in this season of my life!

I adapt to change well!

Rest is one of the most important things to do for ourselves. To regenerate the body is vital to us and the older one grows the more important rest becomes. Depending how active you are will determine just how much rest you need.

Let's not forget the best thing a Doctor can tell us 'get plenty of rest'! The body is much more effective when it is well rested and relaxed. Many times I will choose rest over eating. I can always eat.

What's supposed to get done today will get done, and that which can't get done will get done tomorrow!

There's a time to think, a time to listen, a time to look and just be!
Peace is found in a calm heart, a spirit centered in love!

It takes a good energy to live a good life!

Everything in life has a balance!

The universe gives us exactly what we consciously, and to some degree, what we unconsciously ask for.

Be proud of your accomplishments, inspire and help others in a way for them to reach theirs!

My dreams are a gift of my past, present and future realities!

Spirit leads us to give, created of spirit!

From good I came, the goodness I give!

Every little bit I do is that much more!

The saying is "the truth will set you free!" There are different ways to interpret this saying. I say the truths that you believe to be true, that truth will set you free as well.

Be willing to change in some ways. To me it means adding on to, to include. There are ways of new thinking and doing things. Also, perhaps letting go of or moving away from that which no longer serves you.

If your spirit is calling for change there are many options to answer that call!

Inspiration is perspiration turned inside out, working out the details!

There's a lesson to learn from everything and everyone, always!

We are gifts to ourselves and for one another!

Life is a moment-to-moment thing, an affair!

The world revolves by sharing all good naturally. Forward is the motion of life. I give my deepest thanks to those who have supported me in my life in any way they have. I believe in paying it back, also paying it forward but mostly to simply give because life supports life now!

For me true joy is seeing it in others; I like to see others light up!

Constant gratitude takes us to a higher latitude!

Goodness always rises to the surface!

Different day, more opportunities!

Givers give out of Love. They know that any part of giving anything positive will make a difference.

Create a surprise for someone just for the excitement of it all!

Never underestimate the value of magical moments in life!

Unifiers serve mankind. Dividers serve themselves!

From goodness I came, from the goodness I give!

Joy generates more joy!

As we move along in life there may be set backs for one reason or another. The opportunity to recreate life is in our hands. It's a gift given by divine design. All of nature recreates itself!

I realize more and more the power of creation and this wonderful life!

There is no limit to life's offerings!

It's never too late to change!

I am in control of my life!

_____

_____

_____

We all define who we are by our behavior. As long as I know who I am I am my nature, that's the most important to me. At times it may seem like you may be misunderstood as to who you are by others. Be who you are and stay on your path focused not swayed by how you think others may see you negatively.

Those that seem confident, focused, and self-assured are at times misperceived by others and there's no value in getting caught up in how you may think others may misperceive you.

I can be serious, fun loving, kind, generous, and forgiving because I am!

Everyone contributes to life in their own unique chosen way!

Everyone is unique and different in ways and so am I!

I give thanks for the divine creation of life!

I am a spiritual being created out of love for the purpose of generating even more love while here. I do this in many areas of my life, from my work, to my social life and all in between. I have a phrase I say at times 'living out my life in Man's shoes' is what happens on the day-to-day, doing that which must get done as to how I feel I can contribute towards life.

My spiritual practices guide me in an effective way to connect me to all of my higher self. Knowing the value of these things makes it important to want to share it with others and helping others seek to understand themselves.

We all are spiritual beings seeking the total connection with all good!

I honor the gift of this wonderful life I am blessed with!

My life is best when it is kept simple!

Our thoughts can trigger our emotions just as our emotions can trigger out thoughts, one way or another. Keeping up with them is key to our being fully in the moment.

I am an effective person being aware of all that's inside of me!

Taking my time in communicating with others is important!

If ever uncertain about things, I wait for the right solutions!

Wonderful is Life!

We are spiritual beings living out our lives in a human way, or as I like to say, walking in 'man's shoes'. When the ego is present at times, our encounters are at a push-pull mode making it more difficult than it should be.

When we're at a place of 'grace' it's noticeable to see how effective we are. From this place of 'grace' everything just flows naturally. There's no struggle, no conflict, no unrest. Negative issues of control aren't present; having to have it 'my way'.

Taking time to take in all else that's around me helps me also understand myself, my interactions, my input to things.

Having patience and not thinking or feeling like I have to defend my point of view is it's reward toward interactions with others!

Keeping my life simplified in all areas helps me get in touch with my true self!

Simple is sweet!

My thoughts on the phrase 'Self-Centered' in regard to this book. The use of this phrase can be misleading and even totally throw someone off and be misleading with its use.

Centered or self-centered, for me, simply means 'grounded in balance'. Getting centered or being centered for me means 'getting focused', being balanced.

People from all faiths engage, practice being centered, grounded, balanced, focused at the time of their worship. With my total respect to whatever faith or belief they practice, I'm here to Love, not judge, which offers me more time to live fruitfully and lovingly!

So the use of 'Self-Centered' might be the wrong choice of words in a conversation where 'Self-Serving' might be the better choice.

My days are Blessed because I make them so!

We are all Blessed with a life full of choices!

I carefully choose my thoughts and words!

My reactions to my personal life, circumstances, is my focus. I don't wish or care to control anyone for any reason. I know my concern should be within myself guiding my reactions toward my circumstances effectively; it's all in how I react or even if I react at all, depending on the situation.

I know the best choice in life is to be aware of the energy within me!

Not everything needs a reaction from me and if I do, I choose wisely!

I now am more aware of myself and others as well as toward others!

I use the word 'Mind' all throughout this book. Of course our brains house our Minds and it is for this reason so that we are more 'Mindful of our thoughts'. My closest friends know some of my deepest thoughts directly shared and now I share with you as I do with them.

I am like everyone else learning and growing Peacefully connected to all!

I now choose to see things in a different light!

I shine my light to Bless and guide others!

My mind serves me well in all situations!

Prosperity for different people can mean different things. For some it may mean wealth while for others it may mean fulfillment and peace of mind. Striving to do the best that one can, for me, means first, understanding one's personal nature, well being, and starting from there to be and live within, harmoniously content.

I am not concerned with that which I don't have because I am focused on that which I do possess!

My life has been and is now prosperous in many ways!

I am thankful for my blessings!

_____

_____

_____

When we look at ourselves as an instrument of love, amazing things begin to happen. Realizing we have the power to evoke the most powerful positive emotions within others is more valuable than gold. Going through the motions of life can, at times, become seemingly automatic. Stepping out of that box and living closer to truths, which is actually more meaningful for us individually, requires a personal, faithful spirit.

Touching and moving the hearts of others brings me joy!

My love and kindness will make the difference!

Nothing is more powerful than love!

Envision the outcome you desire to a situation, time and time again. See it in your mind's eye coming to fruition, it manifesting itself to your desire. We create our world as we desire it to be. Your energy and power is valid just as you know you're reading this in this moment. Claim it, own it, and share it as your contribution to mankind so others can set a path for themselves and others.

I now see my desires manifesting from me!

My energies and power are to serve!

This is my life, my world to support!

Life is a gift!

Some people have what they need in life while others may struggle to find and obtain for their needs. Providing for the basics is the primary focus we should concern ourselves with. In reality we really don't need much to be content.

Personally, I say "it's not what I have or don't have in life", it's who I am that matters to me.

I am grounded in Peace and Love!

My true gifts are within me!

I am gifted with life!

There are times when we are all challenged in one way or another. Pacing ourselves and keeping our peace faithfully, even during what may be a difficult moment is important.

This is a very important place to arrive to within. Things don't get done well when one is stressed and over pressured, self pressured. To guide ourselves on track effectively along requires consistent energy as not to fall into a setback when things seem off centered or not going as we may want. Setbacks in life do occur but any consistent energy that is taking care of necessities with the basic daily living details is vital to moving forward.

Staying calm during all storms is key to seeing the sunshine once again.

Prayer is powerful but action gets things done. Even the smallest regard or effort towards staying connected, working to get back on track requires a self-action. With each seemingly smallest detail of basic need brings results which comes through self guidance.

No seemingly small detail is insignificant; it all adds up!

Positive results are found in effort, caring for the basics. It offers a hope, 'a self hope', which all adds up in our favor.

With gratitude for my truest gifts I render help and support to those that can benefit from my strength and power!

I can overcome any setback or offset.

I am in control of my life!

By now we all have heard the saying "nobody's perfect!" It's really not a matter of trying to be perfect in all ways or to feel like one is not measuring up in some ways, it's a matter of keeping up with ourselves and knowing how we think and how we are acting toward situations that we at times may be challenged with. Life is perfect— man at times can fall short.

In time, growth is seen with each achievement— even the smallest detail is taken care of.

Being creatures of habit we can easily get caught up in a routine and not feel like we are growing or moving forward.

Listen to that good inner voice offering you options and good information to help you consider your next highest thought, idea; to pursue it keeps you from feeling stagnant and helps you move forward in life.

As time moves onward I do also adapting to all new things!

I am not bound by old habits, routines!

My life is constantly, abundantly growing.

It's all in how we see things. Things don't happen to us, they happen for us! Our reactions to things determines our peace with it. Accepting peace and entrusting a situation to work out favorable is the best viewpoint to have.

There's work to do daily, a little here and a little there but at times it's important to just take a step back and let things work themselves out naturally. We aren't to force anything in life but it's more important to help things along.

I let life just flow naturally!

I keep things simply!

Life grows naturally!

A work in progress we all are! Devoting just a little time to different areas of our basic needs is important.

We are spiritual-emotional beings led by love. Love is the motivating power charged energy source of our basic being. It's gift giving energy is itself!

Love is being kind generously giving naturally. With no forced effort, just being itself!

To understand and like— to love yourself is to know the value and simply give it to others. Love generates love!

I look for this gift within others!

Blessed is the gift of life!

I am a part of this gift!

_____

_____

_____

Master yourself and you'll be a happy, joyous person! Master others and you'll be a miserable person. Trying to control others is unnatural and ineffective, of no value. Everyone has their own self will, dreams, desires, and visions. Self independence requires one to be focused. Sharing and helping guide others along is more favorable and effective.

Everyone is entitled to simply be as they are!

Joy is found in taking care of my affairs!

All of life has a flow within order!

This concludes the ideas, information, and offerings of this book. Thank you for your interest in having it to refer to and add to your collection of reading material. To care for ourselves individually, as we move further along life's path, serves everyone collectively.

What makes me qualified to write this book you might ask yourself. The answers are: having lived as good a life as I have, considering the challenges we all face from time to time; being a professional musician for over forty years and having crossed paths with many people, sharing in the blessings of life; taking time to think through things for even a minute longer before deciding my next decision about matters concerning myself and the best outcome for all concerned in life situations.

Pure and simple, Loving Life, God and creation, and my fellow man, knowing we're all on life's journey here with a certain work to do for ourselves and others that are following on our heels right behind us for their enjoyment of Life and the contributions they will make for the ones who will follow them.

By divine design is Life and creation— we all are gifted to see it as we wish, as we do. My Life stands for something much deeper than the enjoyment of it for myself. The discovery of all it has to offer is something to be shared.

Everyone has an offering to contribute to Life. For me it is to give in our own unique way to mankind, God, and creation. Giving to one gives to all, supporting one supports all.

Share the information with others so that it may serve them in some way as well. A positive thought or word goes further than you may know, if not in a single moment, but perhaps later on when the mind is more receptive to being open and receiving.

Live today as if it were not your last day here, but your first day in this Life. Center yourself when necessary and re-center yourself to be effective and at Peace and remember to . . . "Love Endlessly!"

Blessings

Luis Stefanell

Love's Mystique

May your days be filled with
the peace you seek.

May your heart skip a beat when your eyes
greet with the one who's in search of you.

May you sense all you long to feel within
a spring of emotion; something greater than what the eyes
can see, not hidden, but there on the surface of your love . . .

I call Love's Mystique.

by Luis Stefanell

www.ingramcontent.com/pod-product-compliance
Lightning Source LLC
Chambersburg PA
CBHW041806160426
43202CB00001B/1